Tea and Redemption

AF632818

A. R. Riley

BookLeaf Publishing

Tea and Redemption © 2023 A. R. Riley

All rights reserved.

No part of this publication may be reproduced, stored in a retrieval system, or transmitted, in any form or by any means, electronic, mechanical, photocopying, recording or otherwise, without the prior written permission of the presenters.

A. R. Riley asserts the moral right to be identified as author of this work.

Presentation by *BookLeaf Publishing*

Web: www.bookleafpub.com

E-mail: info@bookleafpub.com

ISBN: 9789357213233

First edition 2023

Lolita

Her name was Peach.
Dolly rose lips
tulip decorated ribs.

Her name echoed, reach—
for the candy in cotton panties.
Fingers sticky, ham handed fist swinging.

Apple cyanide pips
growing in the bellies of babes.
To sprout and one day shade—

the pool in which her dolly, dead body,
bathes.

Together

The ember tail of my cigarette
lights the way in the alley.

Smoke magnets to your chin,
and my mouth finds the hard skin there.

I know your face even in the gloom.
The smoke inhales our scent.

The embers fade away,
replaced by the ones in our chests.

I am yours
when the nicotine no longer shines.

I am yours
when the sun reaches the dark.

In those crisp morning tones of blue and violet,
I am yours in the gloom to the rising light.

I am yours in the addiction,
I am yours in all hours,
I am yours.

Babies of Death

You wonder why we induce our bodies
in drugs and smoke.

But our world is ruined
and you made it this way.

You gave us these,
and you ask why we use them.

We are children
of the drugs.
The children who wish
to forget your torture
of the future.

We drink to forget
and forget it all.

We are the children of now.
We are the corpses of the future.

We will smoke until our lungs rot,
and our eyes melt in prosecco.

We will always be your babies
despite the negligence of compassion.

We are the future.
But you gave us these things
to help us not remember.

Why are you denying our amnesia?

Get Out, Get Going

This place will devour you.

Eat every morsel until nothing remains.
Fashion your eyes into
streetlamps,
structure your bones for timber
and make people sleep in your canvassed skin.

The manicured trees
will hang heavy with the weight of your hair.
Feet will walk along the ridges of your
shoulders.
People will plant more flowers, wondering why
their town reeks of rotting flesh.

Unaware the silent pleads of your broken mouth,
cries from the very place they send mail through
painted letterboxes.

Unrequited

I am hallway.
With doors, windows, vases
pictures, dead ends, staircases,
but no doorknobs or keys.

Draw me in puddles of taupe
and scribbles of bloody ink.

I am a canvas
you cannot
bear to tarnish.

So, you draw on
other girls
until you finally
decide you
need a clean slate.

Homemaker, Breadwinner

Tap, tap, tapping.
I am the only one home.

I run a bath and let the water
turn cold.

Dinner was going to be lamb
from the deli
and our homegrown vegetables.

The herbs hanging on the window
spice the glass.

But the meat continues to freeze
in the freezer.

The dog is dozing on our bed.
I am sitting by the fire
pretending to read.

This house is so beautiful.
You said it would be beautiful and it is.

Beautiful with its baths and spices
and spaces too big for the two of us.

I’m tap, tap, tapping on the cavity of my chest.
I am the only one home.

Panic Attack

In the fractured remains of our blood
soaked city
we grinned till our teeth stank,
of the tar we drove and walked on.

Our trees died and we rolled them into death
sticks.

I am your city. You are me.

I am your lungs. I am the cement.

Call it salvation, call it proclamation.
But one thing we forget to remember.
We are all here together.

Overcast

I do believe the world could end any day now.

Somedays the sky disappears
in fog and grey endlessness.
Even the birds do not know
where to go.

Sometimes people are so angry
one bullet or blade
could hurtle us all over.

But then everything rights itself
and I have an odd thought of,
'What a shame'

Livestock

Take me out to the paddock
and shoot me between the eyes.
Pat my rump,
the soil is rained in blood.

Hooves chained in iron.
Rainwater wash away
the bullet.

Dear farmer,
my friend, my love.
Take me out to the paddock
shoot me between the eyes.

Hide of ember brown,
wide eyes,
close them.

Take me out to the paddock
dear friend
and shoot me between the eyes.

Season of the Suburban Witch

It's the season of the suburban witch.
Bury your sins on parchment
break your knuckle skin
and mandarin flesh.

It's the season of the suburban witch.
Sing the hymns and lament
beneath a wreath
of violet flowers picked fresh.

Shrimp gumbo, wooden spoon
elephant ivory, gardenia perfume.

Bathtub soup, stirring
until a bead of sweat falls
against tattooed palms.

It's the season of the suburban witch.
drug store wax pentagram
a train at 2am.
Cactus flower tongue piercing.

It’s the season of the suburban witch.
Crumpets and blackberry jam
pale sky and black spires,
toads kissing beneath an Aries full moon.

It must be the season of the suburban witch.
Threadbare stonewash denim,
chamomile tea and nicotine stains.

Bury and break your stitches,
mandarin flesh and earthly riches,
it must be the season of the witches.

Hungry House

Rough, red imitated wood.
Glass splash back.
Smells like the forest and river water.

I can hear someone typing in the other room.
I can hear the wind.

The walls are red like dark cherries.
The mosquito painting is on the wall.

I was young here once
but I stand grown and tall.

The countertop is white.
The kitchen lights are low.
I used to sit atop the counter.

This was a beautiful house
but I never felt beautiful here.
No one did.

The atmosphere is fractured with sun during the day
it is shadowy at night with the warm lights.
Always uglier in spirit.

We loved this house.
It did not love us back.

The walls are red like dark cherries.
It is rough to the touch and smooth to the sight.
Reaching high to the white, geranium ceiling.

The colour runs down the hallway,
over my parent's door frame.
It spills, crusts and darkens
to the red wood floor.
I can disappear into it.
A vessel hug.

This wall is a vein.
The life vein that carried
oxygen
throughout our house.
It gave us breath
and sustained our
daily walks back and forth
along the corridor.

I loved this house.
I drank from its fountain of nostalgia
and sipped at the ambrosia tang
of childhood memories I knew I would make.

But the house did not love me back.

As I drank from it, so the walls took my essence.
Sucked and lapped and licked at my blood.
It became redder and redder the more I
sacrificed to it.

As I loved it—
so it craved more—
So, I craved more.

I wanted that deep vessel hug to encapsulate all
of me.
Disappear me into the tissue of the house,
drown me in cherries and geranium.

Dipsomaniac

Gin-soaked tits,
and lemon flavoured lips.
Grapefruit tresses,
and blood orange vomit messes.

Nicotine savaged teeth.
Razor split lips—
a walking crimson-wet flag.

Ice inflamed veins,
darling you're addictive,
and an alcoholic hag.

Siege

Gone are the giants
gilded in gory halls
of forgotten grief.

Decored in grotesque
gardens of columbine.
Forever weeping
poison petals
in hoards on stone floors.

In accordance to their kings,
in holy bejeweled and humble courts
all those great and gallantry,
lay down upon your war-weary sword.

Gauntlets torn.
Here within ends a war.
Gone are the giants,
left to decay in their flowered graves.

I Still Love Them

There are no horns or trumpets,
to say, I am the most selfless person I know.

I have bled out to my bone,
and used the sinew to mend someone else's
gashes.

Cried beneath a sunken bed and
collected the water in their hands
to drink.

Gone penniless so they could splurge.
Rioted so they could speak.

I was eleven,
and faced my father down.
Like a courageous mouse
would do an arrogant lion.

I watered the weeds by my sisters
feet,
so one day she could pull them out
herself.

I uplifted my mother's shoulders.
Amplified her structures with iron,
and wisdom no twelve-year-old should know.

And later,
when I had forged my own iron,
amplified ant eaten balconies,
that same strength tore everything
out of the cocoon
of my body,

And was shunned
for the first time in my short-lived life,
for caring about myself
more than you fucking mosquitoes.

The Fag and the Fleabag

Women are borne with pain.
Coded in our ovaries,
we begin our journeys
swimming
in screaming vats
of blood and placenta.

A breath and a short whisper
upon Mother Earth
and yet given no privilege of gender.

From tight ribbons,
menstrual cramps
and hair trigger impulses.
Shaved and cut and pruned
like violins and radio silence
never tuned.

Women are born of pain
told to stay in our lane
trying to undo chains
of forefathers, brothers
and even our own sisters.

Two-Faced

Choke me.
Bait me.
I don't want to be here.

I can't be sugar sweet
and vinegar open wound
at the same time.

Stolen dollar eyes
graffiti grin of a criminal
but they see a lawyer.

Can I Sit Here?

Smashed a bottle in smokers.
Picked out a shank
to cut my ties with you.

Bless my corpse.

I will be remembered
by strangers
and drunkards.

Bless my soul.

These tears
are vodka and rum
gin and tonic
beer and wine.

I will be remembered
by strangers
who don't know my name.
Only the things I tell them
that no one else knows.

These secrets will die with them,
like ashes
and peach vape.

Bower Bird

I am a collector
of lost things
once loved,
things never loved
but I give them homes.

Broken necklaces
rocks, flowers and fallen leaves,
buttons and tickets,
bruises and regrets.

I use them to decorate
my nest.

I am a bower bird.
collector of shiny things
a rabid beast of burden.

Queensland

A weed riddled water tank.
Turquoise weatherboard with mottled glass.
Cattle skull hoisted on a rusty fence.
A dry dam and crumbling gumtrees.
The train tracks in thick red clay.
The barbed wire we graze our youthful knees on.

Crisp linen and togs dangling beneath the mango
tree.
A rickety floorboard and gas stove.
It's the damson hibiscus and violet jacarandas.
The dead hollow bones of camphors and the
magpies and butchers nestled inside.

Its home.

Lee Savage

There was once a great man
who called the lions at midnight.
The elephants drank from his water.
The birds whistled when he sang.

His mane of hair coiled grey with smoke.
His hands gnarled like the trees.
His eyes had seen too much,
and yet they laughed often.

There was once a good man.
He gave water to those who could not drink.
Bore arms for those who could not fight.
He cherished every grain, every feather, every
scent
of his church.

I once knew a great man.
With bones of acacia
and the voice of hunters.
A heart too heavy but the softest smile.

I once knew a good man,
who saved those who had no voice.
I ate at his table and listened to his tales.
Now he resides at the table of the Great Lion.

Education

Books taught me everything.

How to live, how to love.
How to shoot, how to eat,
how to breathe, how to stand.

How to kill a man,
and how to resurrect one.

Books taught me,
how to disguise myself.
They told me how to fight my father,
father my sister,
and be a spouse to my mum.

Books taught me how to fuck,
and how to make love.

Books taught me,
beauty in poetry,
and the monstrosity in myself.

Taught me the violence
in nature,
and nature of violence.

Words were a rope,
and an anchor in the hungry house.

Literature reached across
centuries,
and millions of hands,
to divine upon a small, strange child,
the secrets to surviving,
her suburban hell.

www.ingramcontent.com/pod-product-compliance
Lightning Source LLC
Chambersburg PA
CBHW051758130826
49812CB00033B/1199
* 9 7 8 9 3 5 7 2 1 3 2 3 3 *